Shavuot

By Miriam Schlein
Illustrated by Erika Weihs

Behrman House New York

Shavuot comes at the end of spring, just before the hot days of summer.

A very long time ago, in the Land of Israel, this was the time to cut the wheat. Wheat was a very important crop. The Israelites made their daily bread from it. They made cereal from it, and cakes. Without wheat, the people would go hungry.

All spring, the farmers watched the wheat carefully as it grew. They counted the days while it kept growing. They began counting on the second day of Passover. The farmers knew that after forty-nine days, or seven weeks, the wheat would be ripe. In seven weeks it would be ready to harvest.

When the wheat first came up out of the ground, it was short and green. And the farmers counted the days. Then long thin stalks appeared. And the farmers kept on counting. Day after day, for seven weeks, they counted.

They prayed for enough rain—but not too much. They prayed for enough sun—but not too much. They prayed that the wheat would keep on growing.

If too much rain fell, the wheat would spoil. If the sun shone for too many days, the wheat would dry up.

And sometimes millions of locusts (flying grasshoppers) would fly over the land like a dark cloud. They would fly down and eat every bit of the wheat. So the farmers also prayed that the locusts would not come.

When the seven weeks were over, the wheat stood tall and yellow. It swayed back and forth in the breeze. Now it was time to harvest it.

The farmers gathered other foods at this time, too. They took thick golden honey from the beehives, and the first fruits from the trees.

It was a good time of year, a happy time. The people made it a holiday. They called the holiday Shavuot. Shavuot is a Hebrew word. It means "weeks"—the seven weeks that the farmers counted. Shavuot is also called The Feast of Weeks.

How did the Jews celebrate Shavuot long ago? The farmers walked to the Temple in Jerusalem. They traveled over stony, dusty roads. Musicians came along, playing flutes and drums. Bells jingled with a silvery sound. A big ox led the parade. Its horns were painted gold and shone in the bright sunshine. Each farmer carried a basket filled with the first fruits of the harvest. There were soft ripe figs and sticky-sweet dates. There was bread baked with flour made from the new wheat.

When they reached Jerusalem, the farmers left their baskets at the Temple. The first fruits were gifts to God. It was a way of thanking God for the good food that grew out of the earth.

Shavuot is important to us for another reason.
At this same time of year, something wonderful
happened to the Jewish people. It happened a
very, very long time ago, even before they were
farmers.

The Jews had been slaves in the land of Egypt.
They escaped from Egypt and wandered in the
desert. Finally, they came to a great stony
mountain.

God called to their leader, Moses. And Moses climbed the mountain, while the people waited below. A black cloud came over the top of the mountain. Thunder crashed and lightning flashed across the sky. The mountain rumbled and shook, and the people were afraid.

Alone, Moses waited on top of the mountain. There, he received God's teaching, the Torah.

Moses gave God's Torah to the Jewish people, and to their children, and to their children's children. And the Jewish people have lived by God's teachings ever since.

We read from the Torah in our synagogue every week. It teaches us what is right and what is wrong. It makes us honest and fair and kind.

On Shavuot we decorate the synagogue with fruits and leaves and with the flowers that grow in the late spring.

We eat foods made with milk and cheese—cheese blintzes, smooth custard, and creamy cheese cake.

Shavuot is a happy holiday. It is a time to be glad for the goodness of life and for God's gifts to us.